IF I FALTER

AT THE GALLOWS

IF I FALTER

Publishing Genius
1818 E. Lafayette Ave.
Baltimore, MD 21213
www.publishinggenius.com

Cover design by the author
Page design by Adam Robinson

ISBN 13: 978-0-9831706-5-5

First edition
October 2011
Copyright © Edward Mullany 2011

AT THE GALLOWS

Edward Mullany

Publishing Genius
Baltimore 2011

Contents

PART I

3. Silence in the Milky Way
4. The Dogs of War
5. Them Cattle
6. On the Movement of Light Through the Universe
7. Self-Reliance
8. Demonology
9. Estranged
10. Widowed
11. The Abolition of Man
12. Sundays in Ordinary Time
13. The Blind Man's Meal
14. Against Narrative Poetry
15. In Praise of Narrative Poetry
16. Figures for an Apocalypse
17. The Depressed Person
18. Ragtime
19. A Suicide in the Family
20. Fourteen Hairdryers
21. Barflies
22. Ode to the Holy Spirit
23. The Streets of Jerusalem
24. The Birthday Gift Analogy
25. The Orchard at Night
26. Fear on Thirty-First Birthday
27. The Not So Simple Truth
28. American Gothic
29. The Language of Dogs
30. Don't Come to Reykjavik in Winter
31. Nightfall
32. The Jesus Formula
33. The Poet Envisions His Death
34. Blue
35. The Entombment of Christ
36. Ode to Joy
37. Comic Relief

PART II

41. If I Falter at the Gallows
42. Important
43. The Man You Accidentally Killed
44. Triptych for Edward Hopper
45. The Bleeding Man
46. Either/Or
47. A Minor Poet
48. Elegy for Myself as Father
49. Les Horribles
50. To the Woman Who Jumped in Front of a Train
51. A New Russia
52. Ode to the Bayoneted Soldier
53. New Light
54. Gene Hackman's Voice
55. Los Angeles Burns
56. The Harrowing of Hell
57. The Great Refusal
58. Ecce Homo
59. Our Paraclete
60. Golgotha (Charcoal on Paper)
61. No Children
62. What Tolstoy Knew
63. Self-Portrait as High School Sophomore
64. The Revisionist's Song
66. The Horse that Drew the Cart that Carried the Condemned Man to the Gallows
67. Until We Have Faces
68. Algebra
69. Ode to the Squirrel
70. Dishes
71. The Man from Shanghai
72. The Death of Laertes
73. The Faithful Persian
74. Because or Therefore
75. The Book of Daniel
76. Dust
77. I Do Not Want What I Haven't Got
78. A Good Death
79. Light

83. Acknowledgments

for Anjali

Who put canned laughter
Into my crucifixion scene?
Charles Simic

PART I

Silence in the Milky Way

A man
knits

while a woman
who likes to knit

gardens.

The Dogs of War

Two men dancing the foxtrot
in tuxedos on the beach were shot
at midnight, simultaneously,
as they danced, so that both fell
while executing, or attempting
to execute, a step, and were thus
found dead in the morning by two
female joggers who'd jogged
together for years and who'd said,
jokingly, they wanted adventure,
but who now, in the gray dawn,
having first mistaken the bodies
for pieces of black driftwood,
were frightened to differing
degrees, one of them in tears,
the other glancing nervously
at the cliffs.

Them Cattle

The man's wife came out on the porch while he was standing there at sundown and looked with him across the wide, open land that was their property toward the horizon. "Them cattle," she said, though neither she nor the man could see the cattle. "If only they'd come in of their own accord. You figure you'll have to go after them once we eat?" The man nodded slowly, as if he'd been thinking of this, or as if he'd already thought of this and now was thinking of something else. "Well, come on in then," said the woman. "Supper's about to be ready."

On the Movement of Light Through the Universe

We are we, not like
we. For instance: a falling

twig in a winter
field at night falls

unseen; it might remain
unseen. The slow

fog of dawn lifts, and a farmer
wearing boots his own

father wore appears with his
cows on the next hill.

Self-Reliance

An excursion to the hills
is not what I thought
it would be. Our children
are standing like frozen
soldiers, and the campsite
you took pains to beautify
has reverted to its natural
disorder. What should be done
with the leaves that snap
unwillingly? What worms
will we not refuse to eat?
The bears are too careful
to notice us now, and my beard
has grown in reverse.

Demonology

If two
men

encounter, on
the road out

of the city, one man coming
into the city, they

will agree (having observed
him from a long

way off) on whether or how
to greet him.

Estranged

And sometimes I walked
in the garden, which you
could see from the balcony
and which was cared for
by a man whose name I
couldn't pronounce. You
played the clarinet while
standing at the open window.
The breeze carried me trebles,
and I swallowed them.

Widowed

During the previews for a movie
that was playing on a weekday
afternoon in a mall in a small town,
a man who'd entered the theater
alone, and who'd been unsurprised
to find himself still alone, got up
and went out to the lobby and out
through the front doors and out into
the bright light.

The Abolition of Man

See those buildings?
And see those buildings beyond those buildings?

Where we live, there is more gray
 than earth.

The bathtub overflows.
The bathtub sprouts legs, and leaves

the house, and returns at night, drunk.

Sundays in Ordinary Time

Like Neal Cassady tired, you
wait and wait.

The kitchen clock, the interminable
marble stairs.

Someone cheerful is washing dishes
in the bathroom.

You might quit your job, you might
get a job and quit.

A white sheet falling through space
keeps falling.

The Blind Man's Meal

Dear bread, his fingers appear
to say, and jug,

you too. I have located
you. You wait

on a wooden table, and would continue
to wait, like friends.

Against Narrative Poetry

A black knife, a blue
knife.

A red
hand.

In Praise of Narrative Poetry

Into the bleak
lake on the estate

on which no
one resides, falls

the quiet
rain.

Figures for an Apocalypse

In a house at the end of a street of deserted
houses, a dog sleeps.

The sun begins
to come up, or the movement

of the earth lets the sun
appear to come up.

The Depressed Person

Tonight, I fish from a mile-high

pier, watching the silvery

line unreel, hearing

it hiss.

Ragtime

We forget in which zoos foolish
humans cause their

own mauling. A philosopher sticks
his head in the fire, so

what? Here is an earth. Here is another
earth. Here is another earth.

A Suicide in the Family

The doorbell rings. Or a mountain
speaks to a mountain

in a language only
mountains understand.

Fourteen Hairdryers

One hairdryer, two hairdryers, three hairdryers, four hairdryers, five hairdryers,

six hairdryers, seven hairdryers, eight hairdryers, nine hairdryers, ten hairdryers,

eleven hairdryers, twelve hairdryers, thirteen hairdryers, fourteen hairdryers.

Barflies

It was true he had fallen down a well. When people asked him what it had been like, which they didn't ask often, but which, when they did, they asked in an invariably secretive tone, as if they believed no one else had ever had the gall to ask him, he'd say, "What you'd imagine it is like," and they would look away, nodding, their eyes bright and expectant, as if their lives were still full of mystery and hope.

Ode to the Holy Spirit

An overripe banana on a hot
day finally spoke.

Unfortunately, the house
was empty.

Two dogs out
walking

with their owner barked.

The Streets of Jerusalem

A truck now
rumbles

past the spot
where a leper

stood.

The Birthday Gift Analogy

Inside the box, you
find another

box. And so
on. It is only

a joke if
there is a first

and a final
box.

The Orchard at Night

You look, and for a long
time see

nothing. Then shapes distinguish
themselves from other

shapes. Silent
trees galore. You don't feel

as though you
are being punished.

Fear on Thirty-First Birthday

Say the night defeats the orange
triangle that rises and rises,

and that orange is all you say
and want to say but don't,

this Denmark would be different
in two ways: morning would

lack shadow. Indecision takes
on the hearty look of boys

and girls who think staying
awake means staying awake.

The Not So Simple Truth

Potatoes. Dirt and
water. And a soft

towel left for us while
we shower. These

things are no
truer for their

plainness than peas
or pus or leprosy.

American Gothic

A woman with a gun, and a man

with a gun, and a child with a gun, and a dog with

a gun held between its two

front paws face

the camera.

The Language of Dogs

Evening, and people at the park.
Your friend hollers and laughs
because you didn't see her. Now
where shall we sit? The quiet
pinging guitar strummer nods,
he is bearded but beards don't
always matter. Tree here, tree
there. Light pales in the west.

Don't Come to Reykjavik in Winter

"The funny thing is," she said, "my sister was better than any of them. Not kinder, or nicer, or morally superior, but a better artist. But neither she nor her work ever achieved the kind of recognition both she and it deserved. At least not while she was living. It wasn't until she killed herself that she and her work received any critical notice. Though by then I don't think she even cared whether she or her work ever would. Mind you, I'm only speculating. She and I weren't on speaking terms. But, all the same, I believe I knew her better than anyone else did. By the way, do you mind if I smoke?" The interviewer, a man, said he did not. "I'll stand by the window anyway," she said. She went to the window and cranked it open a little, and lit a cigarette from the pack she'd dropped on the bed when she'd come in. "This is a nice hotel," she said. "It's got a lovely view. All my life I've lived in this city and I've never known that the city looked like this from above. Where are you from, America?" The interviewer said yes, he was.

Nightfall

Two horses without riders, but saddled as if riders had been on them, were seen grazing near the side of the road.

The Jesus Formula

What the red grass
said to the blue grass was contained

in a letter. But the letter
wasn't sent.

Found floating
in a tub by scientific

women, it asked us
with its little

paper mouth to listen.

The Poet Envisions His Death

It is true I love
you more each

day, you for
whom I've never

written a love
poem.

Blue

So winter comes, and you
do what everyone does,
which isn't to say you're
uninteresting. Funeral
drums are heard in the street,
and you stand at the window,
or sit, depending on who
the body belonged to.

The Entombment of Christ

Assume a black
dot on a white

wall and a white
dot on a black

wall are facing
each other.

Ode to Joy

The tennis
ball awoke. A breeze

pushed or rolled it a few
feet.

Comic Relief

At the top
of a dune

in the desert,
a bearded

man appears, only
to be pushed

in the back
and caused

to tumble down
the dune by

another bearded
man.

PART II

If I Falter at the Gallows

An old

woman with a dog whose name I once
knew but can't
remember

will appear.

Triptych for Edward Hopper

An obese man in bib
overalls graced the cover of an American
magazine.

The dental
office was quiet at night, but no one experienced
the quiet.

Empty or busy interstate
highways do not and can
not complain.

The Bleeding Man

The elevator doors opened, and there he was, dressed in a suit and tie, and otherwise looking quite normal, carrying his briefcase toward his desk the way he did every day, the way all of us did every day, or all of us who brought briefcases with us to work; heading toward his desk with the apparent intention of getting started on whatever he needed to get started on, his face not uncomposed, his eyes unremarkably vacant, seeing me and not seeing me—who after all was a familiar sight, no one he didn't expect to see, yet who was obviously looking at him strangely and not getting on the elevator right away, the way someone who has been waiting for an elevator usually does, but rather standing still and staring after him as he crossed the floor toward his desk, the rest of the office slowly growing silent as everyone else began to notice him too.

Either/Or

Some of the retreating soldiers
who were retreating because they'd seen other soldiers retreating
though there had been no order to retreat,
died retreating anyway.

A Minor Poet

comes home, just
like anyone. Hugs
his daughter, if he
has one.

Elegy for Myself as Father

The quality of tin,

and a picture of
a picture of
a sunrise.

Les Horribles

In the closet, your shirts lined
up, for days untouched, or touched
but not worn.

At night you wake without knowing
why.

Single people are somewhere too.

Imagine a dance hall where shirts
dance to wordless music.

To the Woman Who Jumped in Front of a Train

I am wearing a yellow
dress, and I am walking

with you toward a gate above
which is a sign only

one of us
can read.

A New Russia

The man had just returned from a journey to the nearest shopping mall.

His horse had been led to the stable.

He was standing in the courtyard, looking up at the sky, waiting to see if it would rain, when it began to rain. His breeches began getting wet.

His flirtatious, lazy wife came out on the verandah. "What's in the bags?" she asked. She thought she knew what was in the bags because she'd asked him to go to the mall for her. She was wrong.

The courtyard was grassy, but had pebbled paths, and here and there puddles of standing water. It was spring or nearly spring.

The man raised his chin to the heavens and closed his eyes and lifted his arms a little. The bags crinkled and shifted.

"Here we go again," muttered his wife.

"I pray for the motherland!" cried the man. "I pray that we not be deceitful!"

Ode to the Bayoneted Soldier

In the woods beside the snowy

field, the footprints

continued.

New Light

The sun is hardly
up over

the fields at the edge of the city

when the city
itself explodes.

Gene Hackman's Voice

"I don't want you as
quiet as an ant pissing

on cotton, I want you
as quiet as an ant not

even thinking about
pissing on cotton."

Los Angeles Burns

A man, or the figure

of a man, can

be seen walking
away from
or toward us.

The Harrowing of Hell

There is dead
and there is

dead. A woman
with no tongue

sat for many
years outside

the city, kissing
with equal

dispassion lepers
and non lepers.

The Great Refusal

Here is a pebble.
Here is the riverbank on which that pebble resides.

Here is the sky.

Here is a part of the sky.
Here is a part of a part of the sky.

Ecce Homo

When the sentence had been passed, the man
who'd passed the sentence looked
at the man on whom the sentence
had been passed to see if, by passing
the sentence, he'd had the effect
he'd expected he'd have.

Our Paraclete

Like the wind, it makes

itself known by

its effect.

Golgotha
(Charcoal on Paper)

And so the soldiers came and broke
the legs both
of one and of the other
that were crucified
with him; but when they came
to Jesus, and found
him already dead…

No Children

When I come back
as a ghost, and try
to tell you all the things
for which I'm sorry,
you will hear nothing
but the sounds of the dryer,
which doesn't mean
you're not listening.

What Tolstoy Knew

We rise and we fall.

A snake moves quickly in the grass.

The mayor called when I was out with friends. He had to leave a message.

Tomorrow is a new day, and so on.

There were two birds sitting on a fence. One of them flew away. This matters little, or matters completely, depending.

I have a question, but I'll only ask if no one's around.

You can't just laugh.

There are hundreds, maybe thousands.

Self-Portrait as High School Sophomore

There are no cars
on the highway today,

but an apple hovers
in the air.

The Revisionist's Song

I.
The archbishop came
to me in a dream. His
hair was utterly

II.
"Practice makes perfect," said my teacher, who also
happened to be my father.

III.
I was a poet. Then for a long time I was interested only
in dreams. My father was a poet you have heard of.
His advice was, "Dreams are not poems in themselves."

IV.
Water moves swiftly under the bridge.

V.
The archbishop came
to me in a dream. He
spoke so softly I could
never

VI.
My father's dilemma:

VII.

VIII.

IX.
We sat in the kitchen and talked for hours.

X.
We sat in the kitchen and talked.

XI.
We sat in the kitchen.

The Horse that Drew the Cart that Carried the Condemned Man to the Gallows

lived for a while longer

and then died.

Until We Have Faces

There was once
a princess in a tower.

A man came and stood
outside the tower, calling to her.

Then another man
came. And another. Three

men stood outside
the tower, calling to her.

Algebra

There is still the possibility of happiness.
A smiling

man exits a huge
park. Hot

tea on a hot or cold

day is handed
to a woman by a waitress.

Ode to the Squirrel

Every time I see
you after you have already

seen me, I try to think of something
funny to say.

Dishes

When I asked my mother what fear
and trembling was, she stopped

what she was doing, and looked at me
funny. I was a high

school sophomore, and she was forty-six.

The Man from Shanghai

This isn't a story about good
versus evil, though good

and evil are present
in this story.

The Death of Laertes

Outside, leaves the color
of coal didn't move.

Inside, two
women and two

men wrote
letters.

The Faithful Persian

Leave me in the walled
city, where the faces

of women I do not
know and the faces of women

I do know are
hidden from me.

Because or Therefore

When I was ten I took a hatchet to frogs.

The Book of Daniel

One morning I wake, and my
television has a mouth. It is

laughing, and calling my
name, and telling me the devil

is real.

Dust

On TV, a woman
with a shiny
face smiles and waves.

I Do Not Want
What I Haven't Got

A man walks into a bar, says
a woman in a bar to two men, one

of whom she knows. The man
she doesn't know is already

laughing.

A Good Death

I wake on my back on a marble
floor in a bright

marble room. No
one is with me, yet I hear singing.

Light

Let the grass
go uncut, let

the drunken
uncle rip the good

cushions with
a knife. What

would you see that
you have yet to see?

Edward Mullany grew up in Australia and in the American Midwest. *If I Falter at the Gallows* is his first book.

Acknowledgments

"Blue," "The Dogs of War," "Widowed" and "A New Russia" appeared in *Keyhole*;

"The Language of Dogs" appeared in *Tampa Review*;

"Ode to the Holy Spirit," "A Minor Poet" and "Fear on Thirty-First Birthday" appeared in *Invisible Ear*;

"The Man You Accidentally Killed" appeared in *The Idiom*;

"American Gothic" and "Ragtime" appeared in *Everyday Genius*;

"The Harrowing of Hell" and "The Faithful Persian" appeared in *elimae*;

"Silence in the Milky Way" appeared in *isReads*;

"On the Movement of Light Through the Universe" and "A Good Death" appeared in *20 x 20 magazine.*

"The Bleeding Man" appeared in *Monkeybicycle.*

The poem "Gene Hackman's Voice" is a line from David Mamet's 2001 film, *Heist.*

The poem "Golgotha (Charcoal on Paper)" is from the Gospel of John 19: 32-33 in *The Holy Bible: A Translation From the Latin Vulgate in the Light of the Hebrew and Greek Originals*, translated by Monsignor Ronald Knox.